CAR

LER

CALIFORNIA

MALLARD
PRESS

Photography
FPG
Odyssey Publishing Ltd

Photo Editor
Annette Lerner

MALLARD PRESS

An imprint of BDD Promotional
Book Company Inc.,
666 Fifth Avenue, New York,
NY 10103

Mallard Press and its
accompanying design and logo
are trademarks of BDD
Promotional Book Company, Inc.

Color separations by Advance
Laser Graphic Arts, Hong Kong.

Printed and bound
in Hong Kong.
ISBN 0-7924-5482-0

*Previous pages: Columbus
Avenue, leading straight to the
pyramidal Transamerica Building
in downtown San Francisco. Right:
a dry riverbed in Golden Canyon,
part of Death Valley National
Monument, where the average
temperature in summer is 116° F.*

When Archimedes discovered a way to determine the amount of gold in the crown of the King of Syracuse and exclaimed "I have found it!," he had no way of knowing that two-thousand years later, possibly even to the day, that a man named John Marshall would discover gold in a place called California and that other men would echo his exclamation as they found gold there. Nor would he have imagined that for another century and a half hundreds of thousands of people would find a nearly perfect life in this place and that "Eureka" would be their motto.

California is a place where you can find just about anything. It has the largest population of any of the fifty states, with a little bit of everything in its midst. Californians are at the same time the most liberal and the most conservative of Americans. By comparison to folks back East they often seem bizarre, but they are also more committed to traditional values than the average buttoned-down Connecticut Yankee.

Californians are so diverse it isn't possible to pigeonhole them, but if they have one thing in common it is a love of the things that nature has given them. And no wonder, because there is such diversity in California's landscape. It includes Mount Whitney, which at 14,945 feet is the highest mountain peak in the lower forty-eight states, and Death Valley, the lowest point in all the fifty states at 282 feet below sea level. Incredibly, these two topographical features are less than sixty miles apart. The state's eastern border is the rugged Sierra Nevada Mountains and between them and the equally impressive Coast Range is the lush Central Valley, the largest agricultural area west of the Rockies. The landscape includes citrus groves and arctic tundra, slowly moving glaciers and active volcanoes. It has primeval forests, expanses of desert and more than 2,000 of the country's most beautiful lakes. It is possible to ski on snow-covered slopes or on deep blue water at any time of the year, to maintain a year-round suntan or to spend your entire life indoors without ever once feeling shut-in.

What's hard to understand about this American Eden is that it took so long for Americans to discover it. Juan Rodriguez Cabrillo, a Portuguese explorer, found it in 1542 and Sir Francis Drake sailed past it almost thirty years before his countrymen established the first English colony on the other side of the continent. The Spanish, who claimed California after Cabrillo's discovery, didn't bother with it until 1769, and even then the English settlers who were beginning to think about calling themselves Americans hardly noticed. It wasn't long before they began drifting over the mountains, though, and by 1847 they had made it an American territory. Gold did the rest.

But even without gold it was inevitable that California would become the ultimate fulfillment of the American Dream. Golden sunshine alone would have turned the trick. With a little help from irrigation, California's sun and soil produces a quarter of all the vegetables that keep America healthy, along with more than forty percent of all the fruit and nuts. In spite of the fact that most Californians live in urban areas, more than a quarter of the state's land is devoted to farming, an industry that employs one out of every three Californians and brings well over a billion dollars a month into the state's economy.

Yet the popular images of California – of golden girls and bronzed surfers or endless networks of freeways with people constantly on the go – almost never include farmers. Most of all, the images we associate with California involve glamour and style. You can blame that on the movie-makers. (It was the sunshine that lured them to California, too.) When they put the sun on celluloid, the whole world sat up and took notice.

World War II put the porch on the California bungalow. Servicemen bound for the Pacific were stationed there and when the war was over many of them decided to stay. Civilian workers who went there to build airplanes in the forties were in the vanguard of the postwar aerospace industry. Developers and real estate agents were right behind them and the population boom of California's Gold Rush days seemed puny by comparison.

The state hasn't stopped growing yet; some twenty-seven percent of all the immigrants arriving in America these days are becoming Californians, and those native-born Americans looking for a change in their lives are considering California as a change for the better. They won't be disappointed.

Facing page: the famous Californian fog looms over a barn along the Big Sur Coast, one of the most beautiful stretches of coast in the country. Right: sunset turns gray rock to gold beside Squaw Lake in the John Muir Wilderness, high in the Sierra. John Muir was a naturalist and author who helped found the Sierra Club and spent his life working for the cause of conservation. Below: cattle crowd the shade in pasture east of Yuba City, north of Sacramento.

Above: the ghost town of Bodie, one of the most complete in the West, which was made into a state historic park in 1962. Bodie lies close to the northern Sierra in so remote a location that its buildings never underwent the rifling by vandals endured by the more accessible California's ghost towns, and therefore its interiors remain authentically furnished. Over $100 million dollars' worth of gold was mined here during the last half of the nineteenth century, when the town had a population of 10,000 souls. Right: early morning light falls on the shops and restaurants in Sausalito, Marin County, that make this pretty town one of the most attractive on the Northern Californian coast.

These pages: San Francisco, a city much beloved by its inhabitants and famous the world over for its beautiful location and the easy-going good nature of its citizens. Left: well-preserved Victorian row houses, a San Francisco specialty, and (facing page) the city's famous steep and winding Lombard Street, whose curves are interspersed with flowerbeds. The Golden Gate Bridge (below), which has been open to pedestrians and vehicles for over fifty years, remains the city's most enduring symbol.

San Francisco has a high proportion of Japanese and Chinese people among its citizens: the liberalization of the immigration laws in the latter part of this century resulted in a resurgence of Chinese immigration to San Francisco, especially from Hong Kong, and today there are 400,000 Asian Americans in the city. Facing page: San Francisco's thriving Chinatown, a self-contained community where every February Chinese New Year is celebrated with the aid of huge, ingeniously designed paper dragons (left). Above: an Oriental pavilion, one of many in the city's Japanese Tea Gardens, built in 1894 in Golden Gate Park as the Japanese Village exhibit of the California Midwinter Exposition.

Left: San Francisco's Golden Gate Bridge, which spans more than three miles. The bridge took four years to build and although Joseph Strauss is known as the man responsible for its design, in fact it was one of his employees who drafted the final, elegant plan; Strauss oversaw its construction. Though the bridge looks lightweight and graceful, it has proved to be very strong – in over fifty years of service, it has only been closed a handful of times due to strong winds. Below: San Francisco's Fisherman's Wharf, which has been compared to the Bay of Naples, not just for its brightly painted boats, but more particularly for the fishermen of Sicilian extraction that made their home here at the turn of the century. Once a bustling port, today only a fraction of the Wharf's former number of fishing vessels moor here.

Yosemite National Park (these pages) could justifiably claim to be the most famous national park in America – it is certainly renowned the world over for its beauty. The park centers upon a valley some seven miles long which lies between sheer walls of granite thousands of feet high. Waterfalls, such as Vernal Falls (right) are plentiful and inspiring.

Boats of all shapes and sizes in San Diego harbor. Since the Second World War, San Diego has been the Pacific headquarters of the U.S. Navy. It is also the home of the largest naval air station on the west coast.

Facing page: San Diego de Acalá, the first of a chain of twenty-one missions established along California's coast during the late eighteenth century. Built in 1774 on the San Diego River by a Franciscan friar, the mission is still an active church today. Below: the beach at La Jolla. La Jolla is officially part of San Diego, but, lying some miles to the north of the city, it has retained a character all its own. Its name derives from one of two Spanish words, meaning either "a jewel" or "a pit" – local pride usually declares the former to be the correct derivation. Left: Santa Barbara's County Courthouse.

Left: sand dunes in Death Valley National Monument, where the summer temperatures are the second hottest in the world, exceeded only by those in the Sahara. The monument also includes the lowest point in the western hemisphere – the unhappily named town of Badwater lies 282 feet below sea level. Despite the inhospitable terrain and climate, Death Valley National Monument is popular with visitors, who are attracted by the natural extremes to be found here. Facing page top: Stanford University, the hub of much cultural and academic activity in Palo Alto on the San Francisco Peninsula. Facing page bottom: the Casa del Prado in Balboa Park, San Diego. Balboa Park, which covers 1,400 acres, is the center for the city's museums, and the location of San Diego's zoo.

Boiling mud in the steaming valley of Bumpass Hell contrasts with distant snow-capped mountains in Lassen Volcanic National Park, northern California. The park, which comprises 108,000 acres, lies within the crater left after the collapse of an enormous ancient volcano named Mount Maidu. Evidence of the mountain still remains – volcanic debris, in the shape of red rocks, litters pastureland in the park, deposited there by mud flows from Maidu's eruption seven million years ago.

Below: the Basilica San Carlos Borromeo del Rio Carmelo, built by Father Serra, the founder of the eighteenth-century missions that form a chain along this coast. This particular mission lies just south of the famous seaside village of Carmel; it has been completely restored and in its museum can be seen the original altar pieces brought by Father Serra from Baja California. Mission San Carlos Borromeo became the residence of Father Serra during his time in California and his final resting place. Left: a Los Angeles clown, a suitable representative of this entertainment capital of the world, struts his stuff in one of numerous shopping districts of the city. Facing page: sunshine falls on the San Diego downtown area across the water from the Coronado.

Left: sunset over the Sierra Nevada in eastern California. The Sierra, the largest single mountain range in the country, stretches from the Mojave Desert in the south to the Cascade Range in the north, a length of more than 250 miles. Below: Gumboot Creek forms a watery foreground to Mount Shasta, a lone double-peaked mountain in the Cascade Range in Shasta-Trinity National Forest, Northern California. Shasta was named in 1827 for the local Shastan Indians. An extinct volcano, it is 14,162 feet high and dominates the landscape for hundreds of miles.

Facing page: Santa Monica beach life. Santa Monica, which lies north of Los Angeles, can boast twenty miles of immaculate sandy beaches and a superb climate for surfers and sun lovers. Some of this sand is protected at Santa Monica State Beach, where picnic tables, fire rings and playground equipment are available for the use of the public. It has been the most popular of the bay beaches since the 1860s. Right: sun-seekers sit alongside seagulls on a rocky beach at Malibu, a resort whose very name has become synonymous with wealth and sophistication. Malibu offers the cleanest stretch of ocean along the urban coastline, with clear water, healthy kelp beds, good surfing and the best shore and offshore fishing and diving.

Above: the flooded moonscape of Mono Lake, the oldest body of water in the country and once part of a vast inland sea. Californian seagulls breed here, feeding on the brine shrimp that live in the lake's alkaline waters. Right: sunrise over Lake Tahoe, California's twenty-two-mile-long playground. Since the lake never freezes, it is possible to fish here all year, while skiing is popular during the winter – the lake is surrounded by the peaks of the Sierra Nevada. Facing page: a Los Angeles freeway amid the morning smog as most of the city's population of three million begin their often slow drive to work.

Left: the State Capitol Building, surrounded by the large and restful Capitol Park, in Sacramento. A city that prospered during California's Gold Rush, Sacramento became the state's capital in 1854 – its capitol building was completed thirty years later. Right: lonely Alcatraz Island, the most famous of the islands in San Francisco Bay because of the high security prison that operated there between 1933 and 1963. Below: Laguna Beach, the heart of the West Coast's artists' colony.

Moonrise over Banner Peak along the John Muir Trail in the Ansel Adams Wilderness. This trail starts in Yosemite Valley and finishes 200 miles further on, on the shoulders of Mount Whitney, having followed the Sierra Nevada for most of its spectacular length. John Muir was the nineteenth-century campaigning naturalist who persuaded Congress to set aside Yosemite Valley's environs as a national park. He loved the Sierra and it seems only fitting that such a trail should bear his name.

Facing page: palm trees decorate the plaza beside Los Angeles' Westin Bonaventure Hotel, a dramatic modern building in the downtown area designed by the architect John Portman. Palm trees are upstaged in Joshua Tree National Park (above) by the weirdly branching giant yucca that gives the park its name. Joshua trees only grow wild in the Mojave Desert, but they can also be seen in the Living Desert Reserve (right) near Palm Springs. It is thought that they received their name when Mormon pioneers, exhausted from traveling through the Mojave, saw the trees as the prophet Joshua, his arms in the air, waving them on to the promised land.

Right: Sleeping Beauty's Castle, which marks the entrance to the world's best known theme park – Disneyland, which lies near Anaheim, a suburb of Los Angeles. Here actors in costume make believe they are cartoon characters come to life (above) to the delight of children and their parents. Walt Disney opened the park in 1955 when it had a mere eighteen attractions – today it has fifty-nine, including the "Pirates of the Caribbean" boat ride, the Haunted Mansion, where "spirits" can be encountered in dark, cobwebbed halls, and Tomorrowland, where a high-speed Space Mountain ride provides the thrills. A monorail is provided for visitors to circle the park and travel to and from the Disneyland Hotel. Visitors are advised to arrive as soon as the park opens, since it takes a long day to see all that is on show here.

Facing page: the Queen Mary *in her permanent berth at Long Beach beside the* Spruce Goose *dome. Long Beach's most prominent tourist attractions are both larger than life: the* Queen *weighs 81,000 tons, while the* Spruce Goose *aeroplane is taller than an eight-story building. Above: Palm Springs – known by wags as the residence of the newly wed and the nearly dead, a reference to the high proportion of honeymooners and retired people who frequent this beautiful town. Right: tranquil Lake Mendocino.*

Facing page: Lake Tahoe's east shore, overlooked by Mount Tallac, part of the Sierra Nevada. California's premier vacation resort, Lake Tahoe lies on the state border with Nevada. Legalized gambling is among the lake's biggest attractions, although during the day it has to compete with skiing in the winter and fishing and boating during the summer, much of which takes place on the less crowded and commercialized north shore (right) of the lake. Overleaf: a rhododendron flowers, a sign of spring deep amid the misty Del Norte Coast Redwoods State Park, an extension of Redwood National Park in the far north of the state.